The Women's Guide to Winning Golf

The Women's Guide to Winning Golf

Jane Forrest

and the Instruction Team of
Women & Golf Magazine

SBL Springfield Books Limited

Published by Springfield Books Limited,
Norman Road, Denby Dale,
Huddersfield HD8 8TH, England.

© Copyright MasterClass Design Ltd, 1994.

Designed and produced by MasterClass Design Ltd,
37 Seymour Close, Birmingham B29 7JD, England.

Edited by Peter D Smith
Photographs by Mark Newcombe, Ray Garnett and Phil Inglis
Illustrations by MasterClass Design Studio
Jacket design by Keith Harris

First edition 1994

British Library Cataloguing in Publication Data

Smith, Peter
The Women's Guide to Winning Golf
  1 Title

ISBN 1 85688 034 6

Printed and bound in Hong Kong by Colorcraft Ltd.

Contents

Introduction

Since its launch as the only European magazine for women golfers, *Women & Golf* magazine has been delighted with the response of its readers, especially to the monthly instruction sections dealing, individually, with all categories of player, from the beginner to the advanced, juniors and seniors.

Their appetite for solid instruction has been voracious and so we are delighted to bring together some of the very best in this book, **"The Women's Guide to Winning Golf"**.

Simple is best has been our philosophy when it comes to instruction and that philosophy is echoed here in this, the first of what we hope will be a range of instruction books from the pages of *Women & Golf*, written solely for the woman golfer.

This book guides you through the various aspects of golf, from the essential foundations that are so important to perfect at the intitial stage, to the art of playing the course, with all its problems. The instruction takes you from your tee-shot to your final putt, including bunker play, playing from slopes and other awkward positions, working the ball around trees and other hazards and pitching and chipping when you need to get the ball close to the pin.

This book – like the magazine – is aimed at making the art of mastering this most frustrating of sports interesting, as simple as possible and, above all, fun.

Most of the instruction comes from Jane Forrest, our Senior Instruction Editor.

Jane, former European Tour star and now one of the leading teaching professionals in the country, has been Instruction Editor of Women & Golf since the magazine was launched in 1991.

She was one of the founder members of the Women's European Tour (WPGET) and is a fully qualified PGA Professional. She now divides here time between teaching, golf schools, instruction days and her family, Jane, who lives in Lancashire, is married and has three children.

You can improve your golf by following the instruction in this book.
Good luck.

Jane Carter
Publisher, *Women & Golf Magazine.*

The Basics

Equipment, grip and alignment

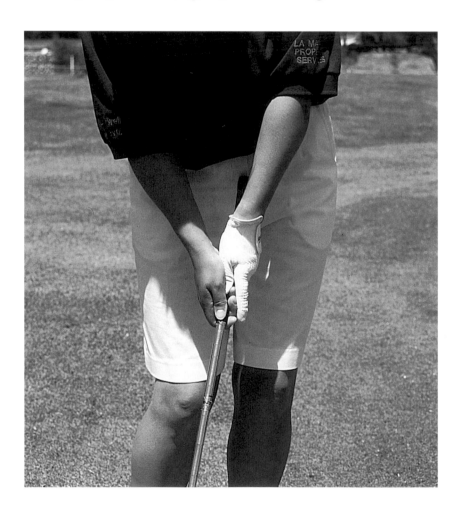

Equipment

Golf is a rapidly growing sport with more and more women learning the game. Before you actually take your first steps onto the golf course there are a few essential items you will need, like clubs, golf balls and suitable clothing and footwear.

The golf club manufacturers have responded by producing a variety of golf clubs specifically for women players. In general they are slightly shorter than men's clubs and also lighter, with whippier shafts, making it easier for women to hit the ball greater distances.

The manufacturers do, of course, want to sell their products, but it is, frankly, unwise to buy a brand new full set of golf clubs until you have learnt the basics. The sensible thing to do is to buy – or borrow – a second-hand half set of clubs from another lady golfer.

Avoid using men's clubs unless you are taller than 5'6" as they are usually one inch longer than women's clubs and are heavier. They also have thicker grips which make it difficult for the average woman player to hold the club properly.

Buying a second-hand half set of clubs allows you to begin playing and to get the feel of which type of clubs you will need before going to the expense of buying a full set.

To begin with you probably need no more than about six clubs, being the 4-, 6- and 8-irons, a pitching wedge or sand wedge, a 3-wood and a good putter. You will need a bag in which to carry these clubs – a lightweight carry bag is ideal, but don't worry about a trolley at this stage.

You also need quite a few golf balls to start with as you will probably lose some. The cheap lake balls or cross-outs you can buy in the professional shop are ideal for the beginner.

You will also need some tee pegs – wooden ones are better once you have good clubs as they scratch the clubs less than plastic ones, but for the present the plastic type are ideal, as they are stronger and less likely to break.

A pitch fork is also essential for you to repair pitch marks on the greens. A rule book is also vital and you will be able to obtain a copy – often free of charge – from your local golf club. Keep this in your golf bag at all times rather than leaving it at home.

You will probably also find it useful to have a couple of golf gloves, which should be well looked after and discarded once they become too worn. Playing with a worn glove is like driving on worn tyres – you get no grip. If you are naturally right-handed, you normally wear the golf glove on the left hand and vice-versa.

Your choice of clothing obviously depends on the time of year. You should have a loose fitting shirt, a good sweater and probably a good rainproof suit. The cheaper ones might not be as waterproof as you think. Buy the best you can afford.

Like all your clothes they should be well looked after.

Clothes should be comfortable above all, but today's manufacturers supply a wide range of fashionable items to satisfy every taste, as seen on this and the opposite page.

You will also need slacks, culottes or a golf skirt, and golf socks, which are cushioned for greater comfort.

A good pair of spiked shoes is essential, even in summer. They are better than the flat shoes with moulded soles. In all cases buy sensibly – comfort is more important than just good looks.

Your Clubs

Although at first you will only need a few clubs, it is good to know what each club should do. Below is a list of the main clubs in the bag, together with some indication of their use.

These are only the irons – the putter is excluded and details of the woods can be found on page 13.

One very important point is the lie of the clubs and before you buy a new set you should have them customised by the professional or golf shop where you buy them. This should cost you nothing. Getting the lie right is essential or you risk either slicing or hooking every shot.

The beginner to golf should spend her earliest days or weeks practising with nothing more than a short or medium iron, but you will get to the point where you begin to use

*Use the **long irons** (1, 2, 3 and 4) for long shots from the fairway, for tee shots where you need accuracy rather than length, and for tee shots on long par-3 holes. Beginners should not use the 1- or 2-irons.*

*Use the **middle irons** (5, 6 and 7) for medium length fairway shots, shots to the green, and some long chip shots. More experienced players can use the 7-iron for fairway bunkers.*

*Use the **short irons** (8, 9, wedge and sand wedge) for close range shots to the green, for shots from greenside bunkers, recovery shots from rough and for pitching and chipping.*

the woods. Apart from the driver – which is not a club for beginners, though not as daunting as many golfers think – the best woods for women golfers are the 3-, 5-, or even 7-woods.

The versatile 7-wood is not terribly common in Europe though in the United States it is used by many golfers. If you can get hold of one you will find it an extremely useful club.

The loft of the club and length of the shaft affects the trajectory of the

---

*The **1-wood**, or driver, should be used for long tee shots. The ball needs to be teed well up, at least half the ball showing above the top of the club face. Most drivers for ladies have 12° or 13° of loft.*

*The **3-wood** is often used for tee shots, particularly where the drive needs to be very accurate. It can also be used for long shots from the fairway, particularly when it is wet.*

*The **5-wood** can be used from anywhere apart from thick rough. From poor lies in semi-rough grip down a little and always swing smoothly – you will find the ball goes further than with an iron.*

---

ball. The more lofted and shorter clubs will hit the ball higher but over less distance; the less lofted, longer clubs will hit the ball lower but over greater distances.

Golf clubs are designed to produce varying heights and lengths of shots and will do the work for you; it is not necessary to try to hit the ball high – the loft of the shorter clubs will do it provided you hit the ball cleanly.

Golf is a game of opposites – if you hit down into the back of the ball, the ball will rise. Try to scoop it up into the air and you will probably "top" it, sending it rolling along the ground.

You should also not try to hit the ball harder with the longer clubs. The length of the shaft will produce a faster clubhead speed at impact, but you do have to swing it on a wider arc. We shall come back to this but the point to remember is that the club hits the ball and the clubs have different lofts and shaft lengths to deal with various situations on the golf course.

With the woods, however, you do tend to sweep the ball rather than hitting down into the back of the ball. We shall come back to this point later and it is not something you should concern yourself with at this stage. The important thing now is to learn how to swing the club.

Getting to Grips

The golf grip is one of the most important of the golfing fundamentals. A poor grip can be responsible for a multitude of sins, yet a good grip will ensure that you are, at least, starting golf in the right way.

No two women's hands are the same size yet most women's clubs have a standard size grip. If you have large hands you might find it easier having men's grips fitted to your clubs. For most women, however, the standard size is satisfactory.

There are three main grips to choose from and you should use the one which feels the most comfortable for you.

The most widely used is the over-lapping, or Vardon grip, named after the Jersey professional who won the British Open a record six times in the early years of this century. He did not, in fact, invent the grip but popularised it through his success. We shall look at it in just a moment.

Several professionals use a grip which is a slight variation on the Vardon. It has the little finger of the right hand interlocking with the first finger of the left – hence its name of the interlocking grip.

*The **Vardon** grip has the little finger of the right hand laying over the valley formed by the first and second fingers of the left hand.*

The third grip, not used by too many professionals, is the ten-finger grip. It is also often referred to as a baseball grip. As its name suggests it has all the fingers on the club and is particularly suitable for women with small hands, including younger players.

Whichever grip you adopt you must ensure that the hands fit together snugly, as one unit. To swing the club correctly and to control the clubhead your hands must work together.

*The **interlocking** grip (above left) has the little finger of the right hand interlocked with the first finger of the left hand. The disadvantage of this grip is that only eight fingers actually touch the club.*

*The **ten finger** grip (left) has all ten fingers firmly on the club. It is often better for women with small hands.*

Taking your grip

We start with the left hand, on which most right-handed golfers wear a glove to assist with their grip and control.

As the photograph on the right (top) shows the club should rest diagonally across the left hand. The heel of the left hand is positioned on top of the grip and the centre of the index finger is underneath the grip, with the clubhead resting on the ground.

Take care not to grip the club right at the end, but leave about an inch or so overlapping as this will help you to control the club better when you swing.

The left hand then wraps round the grip (bottom right) leaving two to three knuckles visible as you look down. The left thumb is drawn up very slightly so that it is level with the

Top: The club rests diagonally across the hand, but leave about an inch showing at the end.

Bottom: The fingers then wrap round the club, leaving two to three knuckles showing.

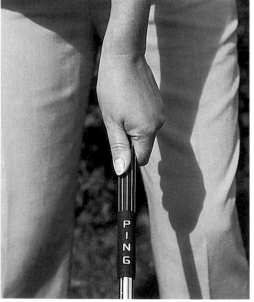

index finger, which keeps the left hand firm at the top of the backswing.

Be careful not to grip the club too tightly as that will tighten the muscles in your forearm too much, causing an adverse effect on your swing.

The "V" made by the thumb and forefinger should be pointing to your right shoulder. The back of your hand should be aiming at the target.

The left and right hands should complement each other, working together as a single unit rather than fighting each other.

Neither hand should dominate the other, which is why we speak about having a "neutral" grip.

With your left hand gripping the club you can now apply your right hand. The shaft is gripped diagonally across the fingers of the right hand, (top right) from the base of the little finger to the centre of the index finger.

The right hand fits snugly with the left hand; this helps the hands to work together. The palm of the right hand should point towards the target

Top: In the right hand the club is gripped more in the fingers.

Bottom: The right hand fits snugly with the left hand to help the hands work as a single unit.

as does the back of the left (where the glove logo is).

Both hands are parallel with each other and, as you look down, with the square clubface at address. The "V" formed by the right thumb and forefinger should point to the right shoulder and one knuckle of the right hand should be visible as you look down.

You should check your grip in a mirror if you want to make sure it is secure.

Both of your hands should exert equal pressure – not too tight! – on the club and it is the top three fingers of the left hand (starting with the little finger) and the middle two fingers of the right hand which do this.

One common fault is for the "V" between the thumb and forefinger of the right hand to be too open, the thumb and forefinger too far apart. There should be more of a crease than a "V" between them, giving better control.

Both arms should be relaxed at address rather than stiff, and the right arm bends slightly at the elbow so that it is very slightly lower than the left elbow. This, in turn, pulls your right shoulder down slightly, which is the perfect position.

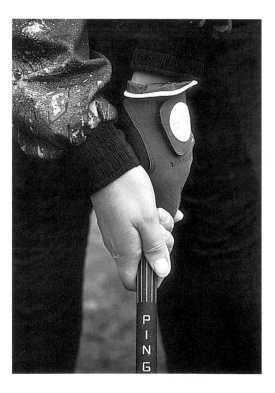

Left: The "V"s formed by the forefinger and thumb should be pointing to the same place – ideally a point midway between your right shoulder and chin.

Opposite page*: A good grip and set-up is vital to a stunning shot like this.*

Left: With a short iron the weight should be about 55% on your forward (left) foot to promote a downward hit.

Below left: As the irons get longer and you want to hit the ball at the base of the swing you should have your weight equal on both feet.

Below: Finally, with the driver you want to hit the ball just as you begin the upswing so the weight should be about 55% on your back (right) foot.

You should fully understand the distance you hit the ball with each club. Go out to the practice ground and hit six balls with every other club in the bag (3, 5, 7, 9-irons and wedge, for example) and pace out the average distance you hit each ball, making a note somewhere of the distances you achieve. Then, when you are out on the course you will know which club to use for any given distance,

But beware – a strong breeze will affect these distances as will the temperature, a golf ball travelling further in warmer weather.

It helps to get to know how far the ball flies and how far it rolls. Obviously it will roll further on a hard, summer fairway, whereas in winter it might almost stop quickly once it hits the wet turf.

The height you hit a ball also affects its distance.

A shot going too high may not travel far enough, whilst one hit too low may well run on too far.

There are several factors which make the ball fly high or stay low, including the ball position, angle of the clubface and the arc of the swing.

The weight ratio in the stance is also important if you are to hit the ball the correct height for each club. For each club to perform properly the weight has to be in the correct place at address as the address position is what you are hoping to recreate at impact.

A correct set-up will help you to hit through the ball correctly, driving it forward – the loft on the clubface gets the ball airborne.

21

Alignment

To hit the ball to a specific target you must first aim the club in the right direction. Aiming the club correctly and aligning the body square to the target takes rather more than you might at first expect.

Before addressing the ball stand behind it, looking straight down the imaginary line to the target – and you must always choose a specific target to aim at. It might be the flagstick on the green, if in reach, or, if you are facing a long shot it might be a tree in the distance, a pylon or a window on the clubhouse. You might not be able to hit those targets – and if it's the clubhouse window you won't want to! – but you must always choose a clearly definable target.

Whatever you choose, focus on it for a few moments and remember, when you come to swing, that the longer you can keep the clubhead aiming towards that target, the straighter your shot will be.

Being very specific with your target and alignment will give you far more precision in your shots and stop you being too wayward. Even when you practise make sure you have a specific target for every shot, rather than just hitting aimlessly into the distance.

The first thing to do, having firmly established your aim by looking from behind the ball towards the target, is to move to the side of the ball and align the clubface.

The clubface must be aligned directly at the chosen target. You can check this by laying another club on the ground pointing directly at the target. Place this in front of the ball.

Check the alignment using the bottom groove on the clubface to help you align correctly.

The clubface should then be square to this target line.

Incorrect clubface alignment not only affects the direction of the shot but also the trajectory, a ball being hit from an open clubface flying higher; that from a closed clubface flying lower. The distance is also affected.

The first thing to do is to choose a definite target, rather than just hitting aimlessly.

You must also remember that your feet and body must be aligned but they do not aim directly at the target but parallel to the ball-to-target line.

On the ground lay another club parallel to the one indicating the ball-to-target line. Place this second club about two feet from the first, about where your feet will be when you address the ball.

If you stand back and look carefully you will see that the first club should be pointing to the target, but the second club points slightly to the left of it. This is correct as long as the two clubs are parallel.

To check your alignment lay two clubs on the ground – one just beyond the ball pointing at the target; the second a couple of feet away. This second club should show you where your feet should be aligned.

This second club represents your body and feet line. It is very simple to check that your feet are parallel to the ball-to-target line but you must ensure your hips and shoulders are parallel to this club on the ground by your feet.

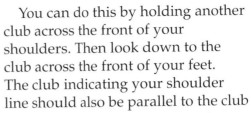

You can do this by holding another club across the front of your shoulders. Then look down to the club across the front of your feet. The club indicating your shoulder line should also be parallel to the club across your feet. That way you can ensure your entire body is correctly aligned and you stand a very good chance of hitting the ball to your target.

If you need any extra help in checking your body alignment, hold a third club across the front of your shoulders or across your chest. It should be parallel to the one on the ground by your feet.

Lay a second club across your toe line – this should be parallel to the ball-to-target line rather than aiming directly at the target. Then check your body alignment by holding another club across your chest – this should be parallel to the club across your toes.

Your hips should be parallel to this club as well, so that your entire body is perfectly aligned.

Finally, before we swing the club, a word about the position of the ball.

It is much simpler always to hit the ball if you have it positioned opposite the left armpit. Whichever club you are playing you can check just where the ball is in your stance by laying one club along your toe line and another at right angles from the ball.

With the ball in this position, opposite the left armpit, the base of the swing arc will be shallow rather than too steep, reducing the number of "heavy" or "topped" shots.

The only exception to this is when you are using the driver where, because the ball is teed up a little it should be slightly further forward

Check the position of the ball by laying another club from the ball to between your feet, lying at right angles to the target line. This is the position with the driver, just very slightly forward.

in your stance to allow the clubhead to sweep through. The width of the stance affects the balance in the swing as well as the amount you can turn.

If your stance is too narrow it is more difficult to maintain good balance throughout the swing. If your stance is too wide then the turn and weight transfer will be restricted.

With a short club the stance should be fairly narrow but widens for the longer clubs simply by moving the right foot slightly to the right.

Every golfer will benefit from this system as the fewer variables there are in your golf the less chance there is of errors creeping into your game.

The width of the stance varies with each club but the ball position remains constant, except with the driver which, as the ball is teed up, is played from slightly further forward in the stance.

Left Foot

remains the same

Right Foot

9-iron   5-iron   3-wood

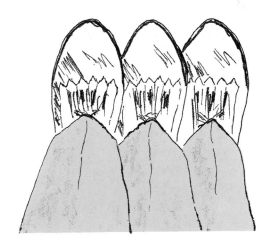

The Swing

The Swing

Having worked hard on the alignment, grip and set-up it's now time to swing the club correctly and send the ball flying towards its target.

The golf swing is often regarded, particularly by beginners, as a series of individual movements all joined together. It is not. It is one continuous, flowing movement and unless you think of it in those terms you will never achieve your full potential as a golfer. No disjointed swing can ever be consistent.

A good swing has a smooth rhythm to it and achieving that rhythm can take time. Even some more advanced golfers lack good rhythm, often because they tried to learn in a mechanical way, rather than building up a short swing, concentrating on co-ordinating the arms with the upper and lower body action.

If you can learn a short swing first, developing rhythm, and then build up to a longer swing, you will become a better golfer. Even if you have been playing for some time, going back to develop your short swing first will help you to gradually improve your full swing.

Let's begin by looking at a very short swing, the arms going back no further than waist high.

Even here there is some transfer of weight onto the right side, though you should keep your left heel on the ground at this stage – that foot may roll a little to the right, but not much.

By looking at the photograph over the page you will see that my left arm is held straight, just as it was at address.

At this stage you should check that:-

1 **your left thumb is on top of the grip**

2 **your right elbow is bent and pointing to your right hip bone**

3 **your left knee has moved sideways, to the right, and your left ankle has rolled, helping the weight transference onto your right side.**

To begin, only swing back halfway. Then check the points noted on page 29.

On the through-swing, again only go halfway. Then check the points on page 31.

Then you swing through impact, again only going to waist height.

At this stage check that:-

1 **your left thumb is still on top of the grip**

2 **your left elbow is now bent and pointing to your left hip bone**

3 **the inside of your right knee has turned towards the target and your right ankle has rolled, helping the transfer of weight onto your left side.**

In the preceding picture you can see that my right arm is fairly straight, extending the club through impact rather than letting it fold too quickly. You can also see that the backswing and through-swing have many similarities. The through-swing position is almost a mirror image of the backswing.

Before we get to the full swing let's take a look at the swing in detail.

To begin with, correct weight distribution is vital and although your weight needs to be correctly balanced at address, it changes as you swing the club.

At address your weight should rest more on the balls of your feet. Don't sit back too much and don't have the feeling that you are balancing on your toes.

You also need to give yourself room to swing. This, again, is something you set at address and you can see from the following two sequences of photographs how important it is.

In the photograph below the top of the club is too close to the legs, the back too straight and upright.

This address position is too upright, so there is no room for the arms to swing properly.

This will force the take-away (the movement of the club back from the ball) to be narrow and very upright.

The club tends to be picked up and the left arm will bend to get the club up over the head. The left shoulder will also dip, pulling the head out of position as well.

Right: *As a result of an incorrect set-up the left shoulder has to drop to get the club into the backswing position. This may to cause a slice as the ball is struck.*

Below: *In the follow-through the arms have collapsed, causing a loss of power in the shot.*

The follow-through (left) is too short. The arms have collapsed and the swing momentum has been lost.

In the second sequence (right) you can see a much better address position, the knees are more flexed, the spine bending from the hips and sufficient room for the arms to hang down in front of the body. They must do this rather than be held artificially away from the body.

This makes the take-away flatter and smoother, thus allowing the shoulders to turn with the left arm held straighter, the head staying in position better and the spine retaining

Left: *The correct address position will encourage a smooth and level turn.*

Below left: *This allows the shoulders to turn rather than dip, the left arm is straighter and the head has stayed in position.*

Below right: *This helps the body to turn out of the way to allow the arms and club to swing through, giving far more distance, control and consistency.*

its address angle. The player does not seem to be on top of the ball as in the first sequence, but more behind it.

This allows the club to swing round the body more on the way down rather than make a very steep approach into the ball. This flatter approach will help you to swing through the ball rather than just hitting down on it.

The follow-through is much longer and has retained the momentum built into it by the better backswing. This will lead to far more consistency in your golf.

We shall come back to the role of the arms in the swing in a little while

Static feet lead to a static swing, totally lacking in power.

but I would first like to make mention of the feet.

In the photograph sequence you can see that the feet have remained static throughout the swing, from the backswing to the follow-through. As a result the swing momentum is lost whilst, as the weight stays on the back foot, the club travels on its upswing too early, with the possibility of a topped shot.

By contrast, the sequence above shows how the feet should work. In

By contrast, as I swing through my right foot rolls to help transfer my weight. The finishing position shows that foot in the "dirty toe" position, whilst I am facing the target.

the first photograph my left foot has rolled inwards (towards my right side, which is where the club is being swung), allowing my left knee to point behind the ball.

This enables me to both turn my shoulders fully so that my back is facing the target at the top of the backswing, and to transfer my weight to my right side without losing the all-important stretch in my back muscles. That keeps the swing compact and adds power when uncoiled at impact. I have to be quite careful not to bend my left knee too much or to lift my left heel too far, both faults which will cause a loss of power.

On the through-swing my right foot rolls to the left to help transfer my weight through impact. The finishing position shows that I have fully transferred my weight onto my left side with my right foot having turned into the "dirty toe" position, so that I finish facing the target.

Correct weight distribution is vital to a balanced golf swing. As in any other sport you must be well balanced at the moment you strike the ball for it to travel on target.

Many golfers fall off balance during or after the swing, even though the address position is stationary.

You must be perfectly balanced at address. In the photograph (right) you can see how poor balance at address will affect the swing.

Because I am too much on my heels at address – almost sitting down – it becomes very awkward to turn and

transfer my weight. At the top of the backswing my hips and legs are static.

That makes the swing plane too flat and stops me from swinging through to the target effectively.

On the opposite page you can see the correct position at address, my weight on the balls of my feet, leaving me balanced and poised.

Being too much on my heels makes it difficult to turn without losing balance and on the follow-through I am almost falling backwards.

Opposite (left) you can see that a good set-up allows me to turn and transfer my weight on the backswing, keeping the club on its correct path. I am now poised to swing down and through impact in the correct manner.

However, as you can see below, a poor address position would put me in the wrong place on the backswing, making it impossible to transfer my weight fully to the left side, resulting in a poorly struck shot.

You can also get into a poor position at the top of the backswing by being too much on your toes at address. This can lead you into the position below, which could lead to a slice.

Above: By being too much on my toes at address I could get into this awkward position at the top of the backswing.

Left: By being too much on my heels at address the backswing is too flat, making it difficult to swing through correctly. My hips and legs are static because of my poor balance.

A good position at address allows me to drive the clubhead through impact to a balanced follow-through as my weight transfers to my left side. My right foot is helping with that transfer.

Once balanced at address, the swing can begin. The first movement is to take the club back from the ball and this is where many people go wrong.

A good address position will allow you to stay balanced throughout the swing.

The club must be swung back, not lifted away from the ball.

At address the elbows are a certain distance apart and through the first part of the backswing this distance should be maintained.

You can see (right) that the left arm remains almost straight – not rigidly so, but comfortable – as the club is moved away from the ball.

A poor set-up inevitably leads to a poor shot, clearly seen in this poor finish.

In the second photograph (above right) you can see the effect of picking the club up too steeply. The distance between the elbows increases alarmingly.

What you must do (over the page) is to hold the right elbow closer to the body in the first part of the back-swing.

At the top of the backswing a 90° angle is evident at the right elbow, though the left arm is still straight.

Above left: As the club moves away the relationship between the elbows should remain the same until the club is horizontal to the ground.

Above: An incorrect movement away from the ball – the club has been lifted up and results in a steep, choppy swing.

If the left arm collapses at the top of the backswing the swing will be too narrow. The correct movement of the

41

Far left: If the club is picked up rather than swung up smoothly it results in a swing that is too narrow.

Left: In the correct backswing a 90° angle should be formed at the right elbow. The left arm is still held fairly straight,

right elbow throughout the swing is vital to straight hitting. If it moves away from the body on the down-swing the swing path will be out-to-in, often causing a slice, and if it moves too far inside the club will approach from an exaggeratedly inside path, so that the hands can only flick at the ball rather than allowing the arms to swing through. This can often lead to a hook.

The right elbow should move to just in front of the right hip as from here the right arm can straighten at impact and both arms can swing through unhindered.

Far left: The right elbow has now moved away from the body on the downswing, forcing the club outside the ball-to-target line.

Left: The right elbow should move to just in front of the right hip on the downswing.

Having looked at the take-away and top of the backswing it is now time to look at the through-swing. Sadly, although many newcomers to golf are keen to learn about balance and the role of the right elbow, once they come to hit the ball they forget every-thing in a mad attempt to hit *at* the ball, often with a huge lunge which ruins their balance.

It is vital to understand that a good down and through-swing can only be the result of a correct backswing – which in turn is dependent upon a good set-up. The photographs over the page show this sequence in detail.

From the top of the backswing the left hip leads the downswing by moving towards the target and back to the address position – but never beyond. This movement brings the hands down to about waist height, the hands leading the clubhead.

Once the hands have arrived at waist height the arms can throw the clubhead through towards the target. It is vital, though, that the head remains behind the ball at this point and does not move through towards the target with the arms.

The sideways movement of the hips as the downswing begins helps transfer the weight to the left side with the inside of the right knee

continuing to move towards the left knee – kicking round – and adding power by driving the weight transfer.

The biggest fault among many beginners is that they try to hit the ball from the top of their swing. This ruins the sequence; the arms will move off the correct plane and cannot swing through on the target line. When the movements are made in the correct order the arms will swing through on the target line – it is quite difficult to stop them.

Immediately after impact the club

Above left: At the top of the backswing the body is balanced, the shoulders have turned fully and the left arm is fairly straight.

Above: Now the hips begin to turn out of the way, allowing the arms freedom to strike through the impact position. Notice how the head is still behind the ball.

will stay on the target line as the body continues turning and the arms rotate. The left elbow now begins to bend, pointing towards the left hip; this is a very similar position to the one at

Above: *Once the arms have swung through, unhindered because the body has turned out of the way, the head slowly begins to turn too.*

Above right: *The weight has now fully transferred to the left with the body facing the target and the right foot on tip-toe.*

waist high on the backswing.

As the arms continue to swing round the elbows both bend and the wrists hinge, so that the thumbs finish underneath the grip with the hands high over the left shoulder.

Your body will by now have turned fully so that you are facing the target, your right foot on its toes. Note how well balanced this finishing position must be.

On page 30 we looked at the short swing and made a note of a couple of points to check at various stages in that swing. Now that we have built up from that short swing it's worth making a couple of notes on things to check in the full swing.

On the backswing check that:-

1   **your back is facing the target, with your shoulders having turned through 90°**

2   **your left thumb is underneath the grip and pointing towards the target**

3   **you are looking at the ball with your left eye and over the front of your left shoulder**

4   **your weight has transferred to the right hip and right heel.**

You can see this position below and you should try to ensure that the points in this check-list are being complied with if you are to achieve your best in golf.

You must not try to hit at the ball.

The downswing is just another sequence of events in the swing, the left leg and hip turning towards the target to drive the downswing. This brings the hands down on an inside track without unhinging the wrists too early.

In the back-swing check that you are complying with the four points noted above.

The lower body must lead the upper body on the downswing, and the head stays behind the ball. Just after impact, as the hands continue to swing through with the club the head and the body turn to face the target in a balanced finish.

As you finish, you should check these points:-

1 your finish is balanced

2 your body is facing the target

3 your weight has transferred to your left side.

We have seen that the golf swing is one flowing movement and we have mentioned the importance of establishing a good rhythm on several occasions. It must be obvious that a good rhythm only comes with timing.

As you improve in golf your timing will become more consistent but many players, of any ability, some-times hit a bad patch. At such times

As you swing through to a balanced finish there are three main points to check.

the player will look for a major fault in her swing whilst, in reality, it is probably nothing more than a slight mis-timing. Just as a car needs retuning when it is running badly, a golf swing needs fine tuning if it is behaving poorly.

I actually think synchronising is a better description than timing, because timing often means something different to everybody – some players swing fast, some swing slow. They all need to have the various parts of their swing synchronised.

At impact the body and hands must be working in harmony because, if one gets ahead of the other, things can go wrong. That often happens because the player is trying to hit the ball with all the power of the body to get extra distance, or is trying to guide the ball away from trouble. This stops the hands striking through on the target line.

An example of this happened to me some time ago when, in an attempt to get extra distance, I was moving my hips out of the way too fast – or rather, too fast for the rest of my body and hands.

Speed of swing is not the vital factor. Having it synchronised is.

From the address position you need to imagine there is a wall by your left side that cannot be moved out of the way until the clubhead impacts with the ball.

The take-away and backswing were fine in this instance, requiring no alterations, but from the top of the backswing I was getting my hips ahead of my hands, and the ball, before impact. You can see (far right) how far ahead of the ball my hips are.

This caused two types of poor shot – a high push when my hands were unable to catch up; and a pull hook, when, realising that my hands were too far behind I had tried to flick at the ball in an attempt to whip them through faster.

To correct this, on my downswing I try to make my belt buckle face the ball until my hands reach the hitting area. This stops my hips from turning out of the way too early and holds my hands on the inside on the downswing, allowing them to strike through on the target line.

By imagining a wall by my left side at address which I must not knock over with my body until after the clubhead impacts with the ball, I can stop my hips from sliding ahead of the ball.

As you can see over the page, if the body and hands are synchronised and the body does not get ahead of the

hands, there is room for the hands to fling through impact on the target line, adding power and direction to the shot.

If your hips are too far ahead of your hands and the ball, you will be unable to increase the clubhead speed. The hips turn to allow the hands to fling through but the hips must not move out of position above the ball.

Above left: You can see how far ahead of the ball my hips are, pulling me off-balance.

Above: This is correct, my hips turning rather than sliding forward too much.

The wrists are vital both to power and control in the golf swing. If they are too active at the wrong time it can ruin or restrict the correct wrist action necessary at impact. Just as a good grip is essential to the hands working together in the swing, the take-away must also be in one piece. With both

Right: At impact the hips are not ahead of the ball when the hands are striking. The hips do not lag behind or slide in front, but turn out of the way.

Below: If you still imagine this wall by the left side of your body you will fling your arms through impact whilst your body turns rather than sliding to the left.

grip and take-away neither hand must overpower the other.

Below you can see a poor take-away. There is too much independent movement in the left hand and wrist. The shoulders are in almost the same position as at address – they have hardly moved.

This will lead (page 52, left) to a poor shot, the wrists being unable to loosen up through the swing, finishing in a rather stiff position which does not allow the clubhead to be fully released through impact.

Also over the page (page 52, right) you can see a much better take-away. In this instance the shoulders have moved, turning to the right and backwards. The wrists must not be over-active at this stage of the swing as it is the shoulders which drive the backswing. Only from about waist-height do the wrists begin to hinge.

The back of the left hand mirrors the position of the clubface. So, if the back of the left hand moves out of line on the backswing the position of the clubface will be altered. This means that some compensation will have to be made later in the swing – either consciously or subconsciously.

In order to keep the clubface moving towards the target at impact the player has had to keep her wrists stiff into the ball.

Had she used her wrists correctly through impact the clubface would have been closed (facing left) when it hit the ball, causing a hook or a smothered shot.

A poor take-away – the wrists have hinged too early.

Now look at the difference right. With the correct one-piece take-away the wrists can hinge upwards with the clubface still reflecting the position of the back of the left hand.

At the top of the backswing the clubface points down at about 45°. From here the wrists stay hinged until the hands return to about waist high.

This is the point where the angle created by hinging the wrists on the backswing is straightened, releasing the clubhead and the stored power, and returning the hands, arms and clubhead to their address position.

The clubface is then on target as it

This poor take-away leads, in turn, to a poor shot, the player keeping her wrists stiff through the shot in an attempt to square the clubface at impact.

This is a better take-away, the shoulders having turned and the wrists remaining static at this point.

strikes the ball. The hands now begin turning, or rolling over one another, as the club continues its journey through impact and into the follow-through.

Finally, many ladies are accused of over-swinging. The advice proffered is not to swing back as far. This advice is more easily given than followed and does not really go to the root of the problem.

Restricting the swing is far more

Above left: *At the top of the backswing the club is square at the top (the blade is pointing down at about 45°*

Above: *The clubface, governed by the wrists and hands, has released into the ball and the arms swing through towards the target. The hands have rolled slightly through impact, keeping the clubhead on its correct arc. It is impossible to think of what you are doing in the downswing but getting the right movements in the backswing will make the through-swing automatic.*

likely to destroy the player's rhythm. Women are not as strong physically as men. They are, however, often more supple and have swings which are longer and more flowing.

This type of swing must not be mixed up with one which just goes beyond the point of control. If a swing is slightly longer than usual it is vital that it does not become sloppy or lose resistance.

If it becomes too loose then not only is power lost but it is harder to swing on the correct plane through the ball. That will result in a loss of accuracy as well.

In the backswing the shoulders should turn through 90° whilst the hips turn only about half as much. This difference can be felt all down the muscles of the back as they stretch, building the power in the swing – winding it up. If the hips are allowed to turn any more then the muscles in the back do not feel stretched and there would be no limit to the length of the swing.

To begin with the set-up is quite good, but in the first attempt at a backswing (right) the right knee has moved a long way to the right. There is no tension in the muscles between the shoulders and hips; this tension is the vital key to a powerful down-

swing on the correct plane.

This second position (far right) is much better. There is a full shoulder turn again but this time the right leg has not moved – it is now creating some resistance in the turn, which will add power to the shot.

The power in the golf swing is created by leverage and it is essential to move the different parts of the body in sequence to achieve this. On the backswing the shoulders move before the hips to create that vital stretch in the back muscles.

On the downswing, by holding back the upper body for as long as possible, the speed of the arms is increased and so the clubhead speed is even greater. It is the lower body, therefore, which starts the down-swing by moving the left hip back towards the target. This delays the movement of the shoulders so that the

Right: It the right knee gives too much the backswing will be too long and there is no tension in the back muscles.

Far right: This is far better. The shoulders have turned fully but the right knee has remained firm, creating a resistance in the lower body.

arms are swung down close to the body and not thrown away from it.

It is important in the backswing to brace the right knee, so that the tension is built in the back muscles as they stretch to turn against that resistance.

Although the swing may sound complicated, and will undoubtedly cause you problems to begin with, work hard on it but ensure you build a good rhythm. Remember to turn your shoulders, keep your left arm fairly straight in the backswing and hit through the impact zone. That way you will build accuracy and power into your golf.

Left: *A good shoulder turn builds up the power in the swing, shown here as the hands release that power at impact.*

Right: *As the player follows through you can see how the weight has transferred to the left side, finishing perfectly balanced.*

The Short Game

Chipping and pitching

Chipping

Having learnt the swing and, bearing in mind the vital importance of a good set-up we now move on to the golf course itself. We began the swing with a short swing, only going halfway back, and we shall do the same now, starting with the short game before we move on to a full shot.

The difference between many middle handicap players and the single figure golfer is often only in their short game. Chipping, as part of that short game, can be easily improved with a little practice. Having confidence in chipping close to the pin takes so much pressure off the long game and putting.

One of the most common mistakes made is to use a wedge for almost every shot around the green. There are so many variables, such as the lie, the slopes around the green and of the green itself, whether there is an obstacle (like a bunker) in the way, and how much green there is to work with. You will be far more successful if you choose the right club for the shot rather than trying to use the same club for every occasion.

An important point to remember is that the method is the same whichever club you choose. The stance is fairly narrow and you should stand with your feet slightly open to the target. Your shoulders, though, should be set square to the target, which is normally the flagstick itself unless there is a large slope on the green and you have to allow for that. The ball is, for this shot, played somewhere between the centre of the stance and the back foot, with the weight favouring the left side, so that you are leaning very slightly towards the target, but only very slightly.

By gripping down a little more on the club you will improve your feel and control. The swing must stay low to the ground with very little wrist action – rather like a long putting stroke.

At the address position the arms and club shaft form a large "Y". Throughout the swing this "Y" should not break, so keeping the hands and clubhead moving together. If the hands stop or the wrists move too much the "Y" will break causing a thinned or fluffed shot. Keep your wrists firm throughout the shot.

Below left: Don't let your wrists go limp – they must stay firm or you will break the "Y".

Below right: The "Y" is intact, the right hand finished with the palm pointing through to the target.

Opposite: The correct chipping stroke. At address (top left) the hands are ahead of the ball, the ball back in the stance. The eyes are over the ball. The backswing (top right) is short with the wrists remaining firm.

At impact (bottom left) the position is virtually identical to that at address but the hands are pulling the clubhead through impact and the ball is struck at the bottom of the swing arc. Finally, (bottom right) the finish, with that "Y" still intact, the wrists still firm.

Practise this as often as you can if you want to bring your scores down. The short game is vital to good golf.

The back and through swing should be the same length, the hands swinging smoothly like the pendulum of a grandfather clock.

The swing should be rhythmical and repeatable as then it will become reliable under pressure. Never decide which club you are going to use until you have reached the ball and looked at the situation you have there and then. Never be tempted to reach for a particular club because you chipped

with that one well at a previous hole. Treat each situation separately.

All successful players look carefully at the lie of the land, the landing area, the pin position and the distance from the flag before they select their club.

To improve your chipping you must first be able to visualise where the ball will land and then how far it will roll.

A useful practice exercise which will help you to visualise better is to take three irons for the same shot. In this example I have taken a 7, a 9 and a sand wedge.

By playing a few shots to the same target with each club I can see exactly how far each ball flies and how far it rolls.

For the various shots to finish close to the hole they must have different trajectories and landing areas. Once you can judge how far each shot will carry and then roll, it is much easier to predict where you need to land the ball. Assessing the landing area carefully will certainly improve your chipping.

Until you can envisage the shot and predict how the ball will bounce and

Try a few shots with three different irons. Watch where the ball lands and how far it rolls.

roll it is difficult to judge where the landing area should be.

The 7-iron will hit the ball lowest of the three clubs we are using. The ball will fly further, bounce lower and then roll furthest.

The sand wedge will hit the ball highest but, on landing, it will roll the

The illustration below shows how the ball reacts differently with each club.

least distance. The illustration below shows this a little better.

Another practice routine that will help you is to use all three clubs to land a ball in the same spot. That will mean hitting each shot slightly differently, requiring a softer shot with the 7-iron and a stronger shot with the sand wedge.

Playing from a good, flat lie is very useful in developing a good swing

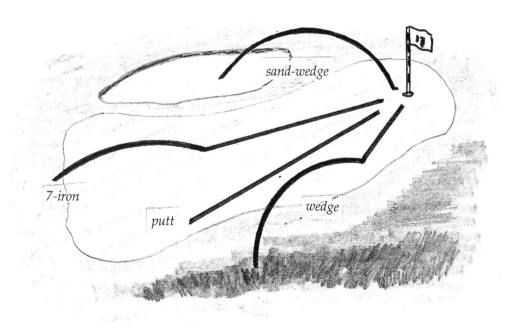

Above left: *The sand wedge will hit the ball higher but it will run less on landing.*

Above right: *The 7-iron will hit the ball lower, but it will run more on landing.*

Left: *The 9-iron is in between both, for height and distance of roll.*

for this type of shot but unfortunately not all chip shots you will face will be from a flat lie. Spend some time, therefore, practising from sloping lies, hitting the ball both uphill and down.

When playing up a slope it is much safer to use the less lofted club – the 7-iron in this instance – so that the ball runs more. You can, if the grass is fairly short, actually play it to bounce near the top of the slope, then allowing it to roll towards the pin.

If the pin is fairly close to the top of the slope, however, a more lofted club will be needed to hit the ball higher, thus letting it "die" when it hits the green.

Below left: Playing uphill will normally allow you to play a less lofted club, the ball landing on the flat surface and rolling to the hole.

Below: When playing downhill always aim to land the ball on a flat surface.

When coming down a slope the most lofted club is probably your best bet. You need to aim the ball to land on a flat area, where it will stop quickly rather than rolling on.

Always avoid landing the ball on a downslope as that will just make it shoot forward faster and you will have no idea where it will stop.

Once you have mastered the basic chipping technique you should spend some time on these other shots, from sloping lies and elsewhere.

Bare lies are something you will probably encounter, particularly in summer. With hard ground and fairly short, dry grass the chip and run shot is the safest option.

It should be played with the ball towards the back foot and the hands well ahead of the ball. The swing is short and low with no wrist action. If you use the wrists you will find it far more difficult to judge distance.

Opposite page, left: Chipping from a bare lie. At address (top left) the hands are ahead of the ball, the stance narrow and slightly open. The backswing (top right) is short, the wrists staying firm. Hit through the ball (bottom left) with the hands and wrists still firm and finish (bottom right) with the clubhead being extended through towards the target. Never let the "Y" which was set at address break.

Take care when considering this shot. You must make sure the ground between you and the green is fairly flat – if it is undulating use something like a 9-iron and get the ball safely over the trouble onto the green.

Always remember to strike the ball firmly, the clubhead still moving forwards as it hits the ball, and keep your hands moving through, too, so that they finish out in front of you, the clubhead extending through towards the target.

Above: Practise chipping with one hand to develop extra feel.

Pitching

Whilst the chip-and-run shot is ideal when you have a lot of green between you and the flag, you are often faced with the situation where there is less green to work with, or there is a hazard, such as a bunker, between you and the green. In both cases you need to get the ball up in the air quickly, carrying it to the green where, once it lands, it needs to be stopped quickly.

This is where we use a pitch shot. In the chip-and-run shot we did not use the wrists at all, relying on the swing and the unbroken "Y" to hit the ball far enough.

Now, with a pitch shot we need to use the wrists a little more.

In the first situation the ball is about 50 yards from the pin – the sort of distance over which, if you are to become a really proficient player, you need to be able to hit with deadly accuracy.

There is not much difference between this shot and the chip-and-run we dealt with a little earlier. The ball is played in the centre to back of the stance again, the hands just ahead

For a longer pitch just swing the club back further.

of the ball at address, the weight favours the left side and the stance is slightly open, though the shoulders point parallel to the ball-to-target line.

Importantly, at impact, my hands are still leading the clubhead. This is essential, for most bad pitch shots are caused by the hands overtaking the clubhead. Have the feeling that you are pulling the clubhead through the ball, but don't let your hips move too much ahead of the ball – in this shot there is very little lower body movement.

Moving further away from the pin a longer shot – and thus a longer swing – is necessary, but nothing else really changes. Obviously, as you swing back further you do move your shoulders more to help you turn. That means you need more leg movement to help you transfer your weight but it is natural and smooth – almost a slow-motion swing.

You must also remember to keep swinging through the ball. Never have a long swing and then decelerate into the ball. Make sure you swing through until your hands have reached at least shoulder height.

Now things really get exciting and we put a bunker between the ball and the flag. Let's deal first with what we term a "cut-up" shot, where the ball has to be lifted over a bunker (or other hazard) and stopped quickly, normally because the pin is very close to our side of the green.

Although it looks a daunting shot it really is quite easy.

To get the ball to rise quickly you need to use a very lofted club – the sand wedge if the grass is lush and the ball sitting up; an ordinary wedge

Never decelerate as you approach the ball – keep hitting through, until you finish like this.

if the ground is hard and bare. The reason for this is that the sand-wedge has a more rounded sole (which helps you in sand) that will bounce off of hard ground. A wedge, however, will hit down sharply into harder ground and get under the ball.

Below: Open the clubface before you take your grip.

Below right: *Aim your feet left of the target and swing along your body line.*

As well as having a lofted club you will need to open the clubface. This means turning your feet sufficiently to the left to allow the club to lay back, its face pointing more towards the sky. Do make sure you set the club in this position *before* you take your grip though.

The club must still be aiming at the target and it is best to use the bottom groove as your guide.

Your feet, though, should be aiming about three feet left of the target as

this type of shot, with the clubface open, will always be hit with slice-spin, making it veer to the right through the air.

Take about a three-quarter back-swing, keep accelerating through the ball and bring the club round to a similar length follow-through.

The club will be swung on your shoulder line, so that if you looked at the ball-to-target line, the club would be coming from out-to-in across the face of the ball, which is why it spins to the right.

Never look up too early and always make sure your hands keep moving ahead of the clubhead. If they stop the clubface will come up too early, resulting in a scooping action.

Now on to a more difficult shot, a pitch from a bare lie over a bunker.

With very little green to work with and the ground hard, making the ball bounce rather than stopping quickly, this is far from an easy shot.

As a sand-wedge might bounce off the hard surface an ordinary wedge is better. Play the ball from the centre of your stance – no further back – with the hands ahead of the club, both at

address and impact. Have your weight well to the left as this helps keep the hands in front of the club-head. Grip down on the club.

The backswing should not have too much wrist action, as picking the club up too steeply introduces too many risks.

At impact the left hand should stay firm. If it collapses it is impossible to make a good contact. Finishing with

Many golfers fear this shot, just because there is a bunker in the way, but it's really quite easy.

Below: The backswing is not too long, though do be careful not to pick the club up. Too much wrist action can be disastrous.

Above: At address your hands must be ahead of the ball with your weight favouring your left side. Keep ypur feet fairly close together, standing slightly open to the target.

Right: At impact the left wrist and hand must stay firm, maintaining that "Y" we mentioned earlier. Do ensure you keep hitting through impact rather than decelerating the club.

Lower right: As you finish you will find it useful to keep the right hand below the left as this will stop you from flicking at the ball. The follow-through must be firm, though not too long.

the right hand below the left will stop any temptation to roll or flick the wrists at impact.

Left: A perfect pitch shot over this bunker. Note how firm the wrists have stayed after impact.

Below: Take the club back smoothly and focus on the centre of the ball.

Right: Hit it smoothly across the surface of the putting green. You must be positive.

As you can see on the left you can sometimes be faced with a very awkward shot, the ball up against the fringe of the green.

This shot still comes under the short game banner, rather than putting, even though the shot is very similar to a putt.

In these instances it is very difficult to play a straight-forward chip. It is far better to adapt a shot so that the fringe will not interfere either with the backswing or the contact with the ball.

Use a straight-based wedge or maybe 9-iron (not a sand wedge) and swing the club just as you would a putter. Focus on the middle of the ball rather than the bottom of it as, if you hit the ball on its equator (rather than under it) you will make it roll smoothly. Treat the shot as you would a putt (even adopting your normal putting grip) and roll the ball across the green rather than trying to get it airborne.

It is a shot you need to play with courage as a negative stroke will not be successful.

Finally, let's look at chipping over a sprinkler head or other small object on the ground in front of the ball, which you will quite often encounter on the edge of the green.

Use a medium iron (possibly a 5- or 6-iron), grip well down on the club and just play it as a putt. The loft on the clubface will lift the ball over the obstruction and roll it to the pin. You could, if you wish, use your normal putting grip.

As well as understanding how you should play both chip and pitch shots and practising them regularly there is one more vital ingredient that you need, but it cannot be taught.

This is "feel". Some players find that feel is instinctive but for those who don't it does not mean that it cannot be developed. The feel for the shot must come from the hands but there are many faults which stop the hands from doing their job.

A major problem, particularly with

To chip over a sprinkler, grip well down on a 5-iron and hit it just as you would a putt.

The address position is very important, with a central axis from the eyes down to the ball. The hands are just over the front of the ball.

chipping, which is something of a delicate shot, is tension, either in the address position or swing. The moment tension creeps in the swing is jerky and any feel in the hands is lost.

If the swing is relaxed, smooth instinct will take over and judgement of distance will be more accurate.

Poor chippers tend to try too hard which immediately adds tension, making the swing wooden and forced.

A second fault which makes judgement and feel for the shot impossible is if there is too much body movement. The central axis, which is an imaginary line drawn from the nose down through the centre of the body to the ball must stay over the ball.

If this central axis moves from side to side then the hands do not instinctively know where to hit and certainly cannot develop a feel for the distance. This does not mean that there is no movement but that any movement there is, is around the axis, rather than the axis moving from side to side.

Thirdly, the position of the hands will also govern whether or not the player is able to develop feel. If the hands are too far back at address they are likely to flick at the ball and will never perform consistently.

If the hands are too far forward the result is likely to be a stiff-wristed push. The correct address position is with the hands directly over the ball as this will allow the hands and clubhead to work together developing feel.

Judgement of distance is also vital on short shots and this is closely connected with the feel we are trying to develop. When good chippers look at a shot they are visualising the swing and the ball being struck, where it is going to land, its height and how far it will roll. This does not mean that you should go through this list methodically but simply picture in your mind the shot you are about to play. In order to create the picture you need to have a good idea of the distance to the flag. The best way to do this is to walk halfway to the flag and look at the flag and back to the ball. This will help you feel the distance without actually pacing it.

In this instance there is too much movement over the ball, leading to a poor shot.

This is better, with less lower body movement; the axis remains above where the ball was.

Once you have pictured the shot your brain has to tell your hands how hard to hit the ball. Without a consistent swing the hands cannot successfully carry this out.

The key to consistency in the short game is the left wrist, which must stay firm throughout the shot. If it stops or cups and allows the right hand to take over then the swing will become jerky and inconsistent.

One thing you can do to develop a more controlled and consistent swing is to practise with the left hand only (for right handed players). By doing this if you do not complete the swing with the left hand you will feel the mistake immediately as you will be unable to complete the shot. A firm left wrist is vital to good chipping.

To get a better feel for distance on a short shot walk halfway to the flag, and look at the flag and back at the ball.

Bunkers

Bunkers

Bunkers seem to be the average golfer's worst nightmare. This is partly due to the fact that most golfers, particularly those who are relatively new to the game, tend to spend most of their time trying to hit a full shot. As a consequence the short game is often neglected. An important part of that short game is bunker play for almost every green has bunkers surrounding it.

Your accuracy on approach shots may, in your early days, not be all you would wish so it is almost inevitable that you will find your ball in the bunker from time to time.

Learning to play out of sand will save you a good number of shots as well as reducing frustration. Playing from sand is not as frightening as it looks. Once you have learnt a sound method you will very quickly gain confidence and be able to play from sand without fear.

It is essential to use a sand wedge from sand. It's a club that is designed specially to cope with sand and has a rounded flange which helps the club bounce through the sand rather than digging in as a normal club would do.

You need to remember that, unlike a normal golf shot where the club is hitting down into the back of the ball, in sand you need to slide the clubface under the ball, never actually hitting the ball itself but lifting it out on a cushion of sand. If you hit down the club will dig into the sand.

You should play bunker shots from an open stance, that is with your feet aiming well left of the target, which will normally be the flagstick. The clubface is also open relative to the stance, though it is square to the real target, the bottom groove being aligned square to the flagstick in this case. Beware of opening the clubface too much and also make sure you adjust the clubface to its position before you take your grip.

Never grip the club first and then open the clubface.

The ball position should be forward in the stance, opposite the left heel with most of your weight on your left side – probably as much as 70%

though don't lean into it too much or you will be unbalanced.

Your hands should be directly above the ball and, as you address the ball be careful that the club does not touch the sand as that would incur a penalty.

You do not actually hit the ball in a bunker shot but allow the club to slide underneath the ball lifting it out on a cushion of sand. Therefore, you do not want to address the ball itself but hold the club above the sand and a couple of inches behind it.

The club must enter the sand behind the ball, slide underneath it and come out a couple of inches ahead of where the ball was.

In a normal golf shot you keep your eyes on the ball during the back-swing. In sand you should be looking at the sand a couple of inches behind the ball, not the ball itself. That may be difficult to begin with but is one of those things you will find easier as you progress.

The swing follows the line of the stance, not the line the ball will take.

The ball should be forward in your stance with the stance and club-face open.

If you looked at the ball-to-target line you would see that the club swings back outside that line and then swings down outside the line, cutting across the line as it slides through the sand. That is exactly what you want on this shot as the clubface is open relative to your stance. Because you are standing in an open position the ball is, in effect, going to the right of where your body is aiming. This helps to get the ball airborne quickly and hits it higher, letting it drop gently onto the green and stop quickly – the perfect bunker shot.

The swing itself is mostly with the arms and the weight stays on the left throughout the shot. The lower body moves only slightly on the backswing and your left foot should hardly move, only rolling very slightly to the inside if anything – definitely not lifting the heel.

The swing needs to be at least three-quarters length, encouraging a smooth descending momentum into the impact area, rather than a short jerky stab which would be disastrous.

It is vital to keep the arms moving through impact with the clubhead, accelerating as you hit under the ball. Have in mind the idea that you want to splash some sand out – forget about the ball.

The swing will follow the line of the body, swinging outside on the way back and down, cutting across under the ball.

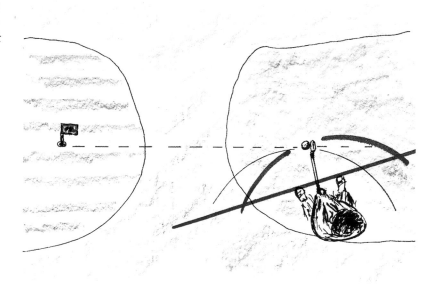

As you follow through your body and legs can turn to face the target – indeed they must or you will severely restrict the follow-through and end up not hitting the shot correctly.

One common misconception is that with a long swing the ball will go too far. This is wrong.

The ball is cushioned by the sand so will not fly too far if you hit the sand rather than the ball. Many players are afraid of taking too long a backswing and, because of this, they slow the club down as it nears the impact zone. All this does is to decelerate the club through impact and, quite often, leave the ball in the sand, wasting yet another shot. You must keep the club-

The backswing is about three-quarters, but smooth.

head accelerating through impact with the sand. That way the ball will lift out nicely.

At first you will have more success if you take the same amount of sand with each shot using the same length swing. Once you become more

Having kept your head still during the back-swing and downswing you can now follow through correctly, turning to face the target.

confident and more competent you can experiement by varying the amount of sand you take, but be aware that the more sand you take the shorter you will hit the ball; the less sand you take the longer the ball will fly.

Greenside bunkers are the most common so you will normally be faced with a fairly short shot from the sand. If you are afraid of hitting the

ball too far try aiming for the largest part of the green even if that means not aiming directly at the flagstick itself.

You may sometimes find the ball near the front of the bunker (closest to the green) with very little green to work with. In these circumstances you need a high, short shot that lands "softly".

Avoid the temptation of being too delicate as that will probably result in a deceleration through impact and a mis-hit. Without the momentum

With a short bunker shot don't be too delicate. Take a long, slow backswing.

Follow-through is vital in this shot as well. Don't decelerate through impact.

through impact there can never be any consistency which is the key to accurate judgement. Even though the shot is very short, because you need extra height (particularly if the bunker has a steep face which you must carry to reach the green) the

Make sure you open the clubface sufficiently, by turning it from its normal position (top) to open (bottom). Do this before you take your grip though.

back and through swings should be fairly full.

The clubface should be open so that the flange slides through the sand easily. Never be frightened of taking plenty of sand. The more sand you take the "softer" the shot, the ball flying higher and landing shorter.

The best bunker players keep their bodies very still during the backswing so that they can hit precisely into the sand where they want, just behind the ball. Naturally the only way to perfect these shots is to keep practising them.

Steep or deep bunkers can be frightening – I have been in some that I couldn't see out of! Yet even these are not impossible though you may want to consider playing sideways or even backwards if you can find a shallower face.

To get extra height on the ball stand slightly more open with the ball a little further forward in your stance – off your left toes. As you swing back try to get the club higher quicker, hinging the wrists more as you swing the club back and up.

Do avoid the temptation to only take a half swing. You need enough downswing momentum to hit through the impact position – never try to flick at the ball.

In a normal shot the swing arc

should be wide and very circular. Here it almost becomes oval, going up steeper and obviously coming down the same way, but sliding across and under the ball, taking a lot of sand.

Longer bunker shots cause many golfers problems. First, let's look at long greenside bunker shots.

Many players either hit the ball

With loong fairway bunker shots you need to be realistic.

through the green or leave it in the sand from this position, something that happens because the player tries to hit the ball too cleanly.

You will find it easier, with this shot, to address the ball from a rather more square stance. The clubface still points towards the target but is not so open, relative to the stance, not pointing quite so much towards the sky.

The swing should be similar to a

Keep your left foot firmly planted to help you retain your balance; swing more with the arms and shoulders.

Swing through fully, keeping your head still until after impact.

full shot but as the club catches the sand about an inch behind the ball it only hits it about two-thirds the distance it would from a lush fairway. This is what you want so be brave about it. Do remember to hit the sand, though, not the ball.

Moving back down the fairway you will often see fairway bunkers.

Hopefully you will avoid them on your journey from tee to green but just in case, here's what to do.

As you will have some distance to go you need a full swing and a full shot. Selecting the right club in this situation is vital. Although the distance to the green might suggest a 5-iron, for example, you must be aware of the height of the bunker face. You must have a club that has enough loft to get the ball out of the bunker. Allow a little extra margin for error – better be safe than sorry.

The secret to getting distance is to hit the ball cleanly, taking as little sand as possible. There are several ways to ensure this, such as playing the ball further back in your stance, gripping the club tighter or keeping your eyes focused on the top of the ball. I find the most reliable way to catch the ball cleanly without topping it is to restrict the body movement on the backswing and downswing. Keep your feet firmly based in the sand, rather than shuffling them down too much, and ensure your left foot does not move or roll on the backswing. Use just your upper body to swing the club.

Always make sure you follow through fully, turning to face the target. As you hit the ball you take very little sand – the aim is to hit the ball first, but don't punch down on it.

Now for a few awkward situations.

First, a few shots from the "Mission Impossible" file!

One situation you may encounter is when the ball is in the bunker yet you have to stand outside the sand to hit it. It is essential to position the body

for the ball being so far below the feet. By bending more from the waist and gripping the very end of the club (though make sure you are holding it securely) this can be achieved and

For a ball in the bunker but nowhere to stand you must adjust your stance to get yourself into a balanced and comfortable position. Aim a little left and swing through more with your arms and shoulders, keeping your lower body fairly still.

will allow the swing to be as near normal as possible. The mind is then free to concentrate on the swing rather than thinking about different sets of instructions.

Swing positively, maintaining your balance by keeping your head and lower body still. What is more important is to keep the head level, rather than letting it rise or fall as you swing. As the ball may well move to the right you should aim very slightly left.

The reverse situation is when the ball is outside the bunker yet you have to stand in the sand to hit it. The ball will often be well above your feet so the first thing to do is to grip right down the club as far as you can to be able to stand comfortably. You will notice that you are also standing straighter than normal.

By effectively shortening the club it does make it much easier to control, and the likelihood of stubbing the

Top left: *For a ball outside the bunker but no place to stand you will have to shorten your grip, stand taller and adjust your swing. Aim a little right.*

Below left: *Swing using your arms and shoulders more, keeping your lower body and your head fairly still.*

ground before the ball is greatly reduced.

The key to success with this shot is to make sure the hands lead the clubhead, staying ahead of them all the time, especially through impact. You may want to aim a little right because it is likely that the swing arc, being flat, will try to pull the ball left. Keep your lower body and head still throughout the shot.

Next, the ball may be under the lip of the bunker, either at the front or the back.

With a ball under the lip on the upslope at the front of the bunker it is relatively easy to get out. Position the shoulders parallel to the slope with the weight on the lower (right) foot. The club follows the slope on the backswing and downswing but you hit into the sand just under the ball, blasting it out upwards. It is likely that your follow-through will be severely restricted but do not decelerate the club into impact – hit hard.

From a lip at the back of the bunker you have a very much more difficult shot.

The first thing, as with all sloping lies, is to position the body so that the shoulders are parallel to the slope. Have the ball well back in the stance and the clubface and stance well open. The weight is on the front (left) foot. As you swing back you must pick the club up very steeply to ensure you miss the bunker lip on the way back.

As you swing down the club must be driven through the sand and then follow the contours of the sand, staying fairly low rather than being picked up too sharply.

Because of the dangers in this shot you should seriously consider playing out either sideways or backwards if you are in doubt. You could even, in extreme circumstances, declare the ball unplayable, take a penalty and drop the ball in another part of the bunker, but not nearer the hole.

With the ball under the lip on an upslope you need to adjust your shoulders to the contours of the sand and hit hard. Keep your head still.

94

A very common occurrence is a plugged ball – a "fried egg" – when the ball splashes into the sand rather than sitting on top of it. The shot looks more difficult than it really is.

Getting the ball out of the bunker is fairly simple and this must be the main aim. The problem with the shot is that you will not be able to control the ball as much when it lands, so it may well run on further than you want. Choosing a part of the green where you have plenty of room is vital, for the last thing you want is to hit the ball out of the bunker only to see it run across the green into one on the other side.

The key points to remember are to keep the ball slightly further back in

A ball under the rear lip of the bunker is very difficult and you should consider playing out sideways.

your stance and close the clubface very slightly, adjusting your stance so that you are almost square.

Using an ordinary wedge might be

For a plugged lie stand with the clubface almost square and hit down a little more. It is difficult to control this shot once it lands.

better than a sand wedge for this shot.

As you have adjusted your stance you will take the club straight back from the ball and swing back down into it on the same plane, rather than from outside as on a normal bunker shot. Instead of sliding across the ball the club hits straight under it, though because of the club and the fact that it

is slightly closed it will dig down more, rather than bouncing through the sand.

You must try to follow through, even though the sand will restrict the club. Hit down and through fairly hard. Never try to scoop the ball as that will only result in the leading edge of the club hitting the ball rather than the sand, thinning the shot or possibly driving it further into the sand.

Bunkers, like the rest of the golf course, are rarely flat so you will often face a shot from an uphill or downhill lie in a bunker, adding to your potential problems. The uphill shot is probably easier.

Because the ball is on an upslope the clubface would be relatively more lofted so you can adjust the clubface to a square position. Also adjust your shoulders so that they are virtually parallel to the slope. Your weight is thus far more on your right foot.

This, in turn, will make your back-swing shallower and it almost follows the contour of the slope. Hit hard through the sand just behind or below the ball and it will float out high, not travelling too far once it lands.

If the slope is very steep your follow-through may be restricted but never try to cut it off too soon –

For an uphill bunker shot align your shoulders parallel to the slope and address the ball fairly well forward in your stance.

always hit through impact as though you were trying to make a full follow-through.

Downhill lies are far more difficult. The slope will reduce the effective loft on the clubface so you should open it more and aim your stance well left of the target.

Once again your shoulders should be parallel to the slope with your weight more on your left side. By

As you begin the downswing try to follow the contour of the slope, hitting through and up the slope. Again, keep your head still until after impact.

adopting this address position it is possible to pick the club up fairly steeply on the outside, putting the swing path on the same line as the stance. As you hit down into the sand just behind the ball you are cutting across the ball as well, so getting it up quickly. There is a danger, though, of coming up too soon and thus thinning the shot. To avoid this shuffle your feet further down into the sand so that you are a little lower relative to the ball and drive the club through impact, again following the contour of the sand rather than lifting the club up too quickly in the follow-through.

Again, restrict your lower body movement in the backswing and downswing, only turning to face the target after impact. Keep your head very still through the shot, until after impact. That will help you make this a successful recovery.

Think carefully before you do anything when faced with a difficult shot from a bunker.

Be certain of what you are trying to do and what you can do – don't waste any shots experimenting on the course – do that on the practice ground.

If you want to be a good bunker player you must practise in bunkers. There is no short cut to success.

Hitting from a downslope in a bunker is very difficult and you will have little chance of controlling the ball once it lands. Have the clubface open, take the club back up steeply and swing down and along the contours of the slope, hitting firmly. You are always hitting across the ball-to-target line. Keep your head still until after impact.

Putting Skills

Putting Skills

Putting makes a vast difference to any golfer's score. The golf scoring system dictates that on most golf courses you should take thirty-six putts if you are achieving par. Most of us would be happy with thirty putts per round but it is all too easy to run up forty or more.

Obviously the closer you can get the ball with your approach shot the more likely you are to hole the putt, but with a good putting stroke and sufficient confidence there is a very good chance of salvaging a par or achieving a birdie. Also, if you can develop a good putting action you will be able to cut out virtually all those costly three-putts. On the greens it is easy to save up to half a dozen strokes – a big difference to your overall score.

The key to putting is consistency. A smooth swing and rhythm will help with judgement of distance, thus developing a "feel" for putts.

There are two different methods of putting, tapping the ball or rolling the ball. The woman who taps the ball tends to have a very wristy style and to stop the putter at impact. This has been very successful for many good golfers, including Arnold Palmer and Gary Player. More players tended to tap the ball when greens were not as fast as they are in tournament golf today. Certainly in the winter when greens are not cut as often as they are in summer, leaving the grass slightly longer, it is more difficult to roll the ball with the same confidence as in the summer on very short grass.

Rolling the ball is achieved by a smooth swing from the shoulders with no wrist action at all. The idea is to put top spin on the ball which will make it roll and stay on line. Most of the top tournament players, men and women, use this method and it is this one I strongly recommend.

Before we get on to learning the skills involved in putting it is worth just reminding you of a couple of points about etiquette and the rules on the green.

Etiquette is, basically, consideration for others. This includes staying quiet and still whilst someone else is putting or preparing to putt and never walking on the line of someone else's putt.

The order of play on the green is just as it is on the fairway – the player whose ball is furthest from the hole plays first.

If asked to tend the flag avoid casting a shadow across the hole and furl the flag to stop it waving in any wind.

When you are putting on the green you may have the flag taken out (in which case it is a good idea to lay it down off the green where it will not be hit by any ball being putted) or attended, your opponent or partner holding it. The best way to hold it is to gather the flag in your hand so that

When marking the ball make sure you place the marker behind it and be careful not to move the ball.

it does not flap about in any wind, and also to be sure to stand so that you never cast a shadow across the hole. If you leave the flagstick in and strike it with your ball you incur a two-stroke penalty in strokeplay and the loss of the hole in matchplay.

It is up to the person putting to decide whether the flag should be taken out or attended. If you are putting from off the green you may leave the flagstick in – there is no penalty if you strike it.

It is also possible, on the green, to mark your ball, lifting it (and cleaning it if you wish), either because it is on the line of your opponent's putt, or just because you wish to. If your opponent's ball is, in your opinion, close to your line and you are fearful of hitting it (a penalty in strokeplay) you can ask for that to be marked as well. Marking its position correctly is essential.

Ball markers can be any small round object. You can use a small coin or buy a special ball marker. Place this directly behind the ball in line with the flagstick and then carefully remove your ball.

When you come to replace the ball put that down first, ahead of the marker, then carefully remove the marker.

There may be occasions when your marker is on or close to the line of your opponent's putt. In this case you are allowed (and may be asked) to move your marker. To do this, having marked the position of your ball first, align your putter head from the marker to some easily identifiable and

If you need to move your marker align the putter head on some immovable object, like a tree.

immovable object (a tree perhaps) off the green. Move the marker to the far end of the putter head. Don't forget to move it back again before you replace the ball.

Getting these things correct may not help you to become a better putter but it will increase your knowledge of golf, for nothing is more disconcerting than being unsure of the rules in certain circumstances.

In the reverse overlap putting grip the little finger of the right hand merely changes place with the left forefinger.

The putting grip is different from the normal golf grip. Most of today's better players use what is known as a reverse overlap grip.

It is very similar to the Vardon grip, described much earlier, with the difference being that the index finger of the left hand and the small finger of the right hand change places. In the Vardon grip the little finger of the right hand overlaps the index finger

A narrow stance will help you as you do not want any lower body or leg movement.

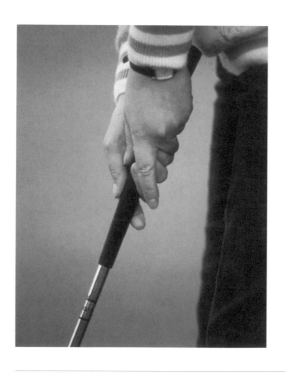

of the left. To putt consistently well, just reverse these two fingers.

The left index finger can then point down the left side of the shaft, helping to balance the putter better and to keep the wrists firm through impact. That is important.

A narrow stance helps to keep the body still as any body movement is easily noticed. In a wind a slightly wider stance will help you to maintain good balance.

It would be wonderful to be as accurate in putting as snooker players are in their game. Of course snooker tables are perfectly flat but they also have another advantage denied golfers. They can get their eyes directly behind the cue ball, looking directly down the target line.

Golfers have to stand to putt and more than that, they have to stand to one side of the ball and putt sideways. We can, however, make sure that our eyes are directly above the target line. To check this there are two things you can do.

Top right: By dropping a ball from the bridge of your nose you can check that your eyes are directly above the ball on the ground.

Right: You could also do this by hanging the putter from the same place. It should be directly over the ball.

First, set up to your normal putting position with the ball midway in your stance. Hold a second ball on the bridge of your nose and drop it. It should hit the ball which is on the ground. If it does, your eyes are directly above the ball. If it misses, adjust your position until the dropping ball does hit the one on the ground.

Another way to do this, and perhaps one that is slightly simpler, is to hold the putter with the top of the shaft resting on the bridge of your nose. If the putter head hides the ball you have the correct position.

The putting stroke must, above all, be smooth, with the arms, hands and putter moving as a single unit.

Before you putt you must also make sure you are aiming at the hole, or your target on a sloping green, something we shall come to in a few moments.

Imagining that for the moment we have a flat putting green you must have the putter face absolutely square to the target if you are to stand a chance of holing the putt.

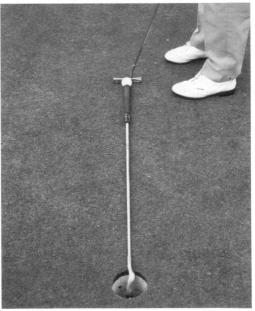

Top right: *Make a channel for yourself to putt along on short putts.*

Right: *The putter face must be absolutely square to the target if you are to putt well.*

On the practice green lay two clubs down pointing to either side of the hole so that you have a channel through which to putt the ball.
At the end of the channel the ball will just drop in the hole.

Many golfers fail to align their feet and shoulders parallel to this target line. To learn better putting have everything aligned correctly.

At address (below) your arms and the putter shaft form a large "Y". Throughout the putting stroke that "Y" never changes shape – it just swings from side to side.

Far too many players use their hands and wrists too much in the putting stroke. What you need to remember is that the wrists stay locked firm – almost as if you had a splint binding them together.

By cutting out wrist movement you improve your putting stroke.

The shoulders and arms move, but

You should just feel a gentle rocking of the shoulders in a good putt.

again as a single unit, swinging almost pendulum-like whilst the head remains perfectly still.

Think of a large "Y" formed by the arms and the putter shaft. Although the tail of this "Y" moves the shape never alters – it just swings from side to side hanging from your shoulders.

Think that on the backswing the left shoulder moves and on the through-swing the right shoulder moves. It is not, however, a big turn as in a full swing but just a gentle rocking on the inside of the shoulders.

The putter swings on a slight arc on the backswing due to the movement of the shoulders. trying to swing too straight back on the backswing may result in closing the putter face.

By learning to swing the putter in this way you will find it easier to roll the ball, which will then hold its line better and run more smoothly.

Another major fault in putting is the deceleration of the putter head as it hits the ball. To achieve consistently good putting you must continue the stroke right through to the end, the putter head staying almost square to the target throughout and finishing pointing at the hole itself.

Putting, unlike other shots, needs no leg or lower body movement. When learning, stand perfectly square

but as you progress you may adopt a different stance. Just make sure your shoulders are square to the target. Do check, also, that the putter head is square to the target.

The back and through swings should be the same length and you must keep your arms and wrists firm, though not rigid, throughout the stroke. Finish with the hands and putter aiming at the target.

Having learnt the basic putting stroke it is time to move on to the sort of situations you will find on the golf course. On the green your first putt is likely to be a fairly long one. Getting the direction correct is important but getting the distance correct is vital. Very rarely does a mistake in choice of direction cause a three-putt. It is far more common to misjudge distance than direction.

Left, top line: Have three balls in a row. Putt the first, check the distance then putt the other two without looking up.

Bottom left: Roll the ball to the hole as that will help with your judgement of distance.

Bottom right: Walk halfway to the flagstick. It helps you with gradients too.

Judgement of distance is vital from long range and without it you will struggle to become a good player. With an accurate first putt, which may be coming to a halt very close to the pin, the ball does stand a chance of dropping in.

There is only one way to improve your long putting skills – practise!

Have three balls in a line on the putting green and judge the distance normally. Strike the first one, watch where it finishes and then hit the next two balls without looking at the hole. This will teach you "feel", so that you can begin to understand how hard you hit the ball. You are focusing your concentration on the feel of the shot rather than on the visual aspect.

It may take you some time to get this right but it is an excellent drill and one that Tom Watson uses.

A second way to judge distance is by rolling a ball towards the hole. You get the feel of how hard you have to roll it as you extend your arm and hand through towards the target. Then use that knowledge with a putter, extending your putter through about the same amount.

Thirdly, get to understand the distance to the hole by walking to a point about halfway between your ball and the hole. Take a practice "putt" from that position and then walk back to your ball. It will give you a good idea of the overall distance. This exercise is particularly useful on a sloping green where you might not realise quite how steep the gradient is. Walking up it makes you aware of the slope.

Don't look up – it is often said that, on a short putt, you should hear the ball drop, not see it.

Finally, short putts which some players often miss because they fail to take enough care over them.

Many short putts are missed because the player looks up too quickly. This often causes a putt to be missed on the left of the hole.

Equally common is the fault caused by the left wrist collapsing at impact.

Putt with your left hand only – that will make you keep that wrist firm.

Keep as still as you can whilst putting; body movement like this is the main cause of missed putts.

Try putting with your left hand only. If your left wrist collapses the ball will not roll to the hole correctly.

You must keep the back of your left wrist moving towards the hole all the time.

One of the main causes of short putts being missed is unnecessary body movement. Only the shoulders, arms and hands move, and then all together as a single unit. If the body sways the putter cannot hold its line. Hold your finish to check whether or not the putter face and back of the left hand are still square to the target, which they should be.

Something else which may help you is to keep your left wrist a little higher at address, which will force you to keep it firmer. You must, though, make sure your hands are still working together as a single unit, which will be helped by the reverse overlap grip.

Putting is something you must practise as often as possible. If you do you will soon stop wasting shots.

Hold your left hand a little higher at address, but keep both hands as a single unit.

Woods & Long Irons

The woods

The first shot you hit in any round of golf will be a tee-shot. Although not every golfer should use the driver every time it is a club you should get to know and use well. The driver is not, however, the only wood and I suggest that when you first begin playing you use the 5-wood, which is not very much longer than the mid-irons and has plenty of loft to get the ball up in the air.

Many golfers think they should swing differently with a wood but this is not so. The swing is the same. Just because a wood will normally hit the ball further than an iron it does not mean that you have to swing it faster.

The shaft on a wood is longer than the shaft on an equivalent iron, which is why it goes further. Yet the club-head needs more time to catch up with the hands and the turn of the body. Also, because the shaft is longer the angle of attack into the ball is shallower. You do not have to do anything to change that angle of attack – the length of the shaft makes you stand slightly further from the ball and it happens without you thinking about it.

You must, however, have in mind a sweeping motion through the ball rather than a downward hit as happens with shorter irons.

The best shot with a wood is one where the clubhead spends most time close to the ground, sweeping through on a low, wide arc rather than swinging down and up.

Tempo is vital to good wood play.

If you have the ball on a tee you should not try to hit it up into the air – just concentrate on hitting it forward. The loft on the face of the wood (even on a driver) is sufficient to get the ball airborne. Don't try to hit down; don't try to hit up. Hit it forward.

Ball position is important and you should have the ball just inside your left heel.

As you turn on the full backswing your weight moves to your right side. Although your left heel may rise slightly you must keep the outside edge of the left foot on the ground.

Never be too concerned with length when you hit a wood. The more you try to force distance the less likely you are to get it. Hitting the shot solidly will make it go further and good tempo is vital to this.

There are three basic moves in the swing that you should remember:

Don't have the ball too far back in your stance.

1 **turn your top half away from the target on the backswing**

2 **to start the downswing turn your hips sideways towards the target and your hands will drop to waist height**

3 **swing your arms through freely.**

Turn fully, rolling your left heel rather than raising it.

Many golfers are often so keen to get through the ball that they forget to swing in a co-ordinated manner. The hips should lead the arms and hands on the downswing but it is very important that the arms and hands follow closely.

Don't let the hands drag too far behind as they have to swish the clubhead through, releasing the

power at impact. If the arms get left behind the clubhead will as well.

Although you will find it easier to use the 5-wood to begin with (even from the tee) you will soon gain confidence to move up to the 3-wood and driver. Getting to know them well will benefit you enormously.

When you have the ball on a tee-peg don't try to hit the ball up – just

Don't let your top half get ahead of your hands.

This is how you should be at impact, your head behind the ball.

Finish facing the target, your weight on your left side.

Long irons

Now for long irons, which cause so many problems. They are definitely not the easiest clubs in the bag to use yet you have them so you might as well learn to use them.

Some clubs are easier to use than others, the peripherally weighted clubs (like Ping) being more forgiving than a traditional blade.

concentrate on hitting it forwards. It is often a good idea to imagine you have another ball a foot in front of the real ball. Your aim should be to hit this imaginary ball as you hit through.

Teeing the ball the correct height is important, but too many ladies tee it too low, worrying, perhaps, about skying the shot. In fact, the lower you tee the ball the more likely you are to sky it because, being too low, you subconsciously try to hit down at it whereas you must hit through it.

You need a low, sweeping action to hit long irons well, just as with the woods. For this reason you must not have the ball too far back in the stance or it will force you into too steep a take-away. You should almost feel that you drag the club back along the ground in the first part of the backswing. From there swing normally, keeping the clubhead low to the ground on the take-away, turning fully with the shoulders, your back facing the target at the top of the backswing, then turn the hips to the left, dragging the arms down which in turn are pulling the club.

Again you want a long and low swing through the ball, turning to a full follow-through. Never rush it, never try to hit harder, never try to scoop the ball up into the air. Hit it forward. The clubface will do the rest.

Never imagine that every club has a different swing. The swing remains the same. The only things that change are the stance (normally wider with a longer iron or wood) and the distance you stand from the ball, because of the length of the shaft. A longer shaft makes you swing flatter but it should be subconscious.

Concentrate only on turning fully and hitting through the impact zone into a full follow-through.

Left: *A perfect impact position with a long iron – the hands have released the club-head yet have not overtaken it.*

Right: I*t is vital to follow through fully on these shots if you are to hit the ball a good distance accurately. The club is staying low.*

Trouble shots

Slopes; working the ball;
playing from rough

Slopes

It is rare to find a golf course that is totally flat so learning to play from sloping lies is essential. Although many ladies are unsure how to play these shots they are, with just a few minor adjustments, easy.

We begin with uphill lies. The ball will fly higher from an uphill lie though be aware that if it flies higher it will normally go less distance. Club selection is therefore vital; a 5-iron might be needed when normally a 7-iron would carry the distance.

Make sure you stand perpendicular to the slope with most of your weight on your lower foot – the right in this case. You also need to adjust your

Below left: *For an uphill shot you need to stand perpendicular to the slope, your weight on your lower foot.*

Below: *For a downhill shot the opposite is true.*

alignment, aiming a little to the right of where you want the ball to finish as it will draw to the left in flight.

Keep your body fairly still throughout the backswing and downswing, being careful not to fall onto the lower foot. As you hit the ball continue the through-swing up the slope, keeping

the clubhead fairly low to the ground.

For downhill lies the opposite applies. Your weight is more on your front (left) foot and you should aim to the left as the ball will fade during flight. The ball will fly lower and longer from a downhill lie so you will need less club for the distance.

With the ball above your feet grip down the club more and stand more upright. Your weight is more on your toes.

With the ball below your feet you should be more balanced on your heels and also bend your knees more.

Keep very still on the backswing and follow the clubhead through the shot, down the hill, as you swing.

With the ball above your feet you should push your weight into the slope, so that you are more on your toes – never allow yourself to fall back onto your heels. Your legs will be straighter although you should still bend from the hips. You should grip further down on the club. As you swing make sure you maintain your balance, so don't overswing.

As your swing will be flatter than normal (because of your stance) the ball will hook from this position so you should aim a little more to the right. You will need less club for this shot than normal.

With the ball below your feet you must guard against toppling over down the slope. To counteract this stand with your legs more flexed, though not too big a bend from the hips. Try to keep your spine fairly straight. The ball is likely to fade so aim more to the left and ideally take more club.

For all shots from sloping lies the secret is to stay balanced and follow the slope, the clubhead swinging through on the contours as long as possible. Never overswing and keep your head and lower body fairly still until after impact.

Shaping your shots

Whilst hitting the ball straight is every golfer's ideal, there are occasions when you need to be able to work the ball, shaping your shots to get round, over or under some obstruction.

Let's begin with the fade, a shot which moves left to right in the air. One problem many golfers encounter is in trying to adjust their swing to shape their shots. This is wrong. You merely adjust your set-up.

Rather than being aligned parallel to the target line, stand with your feet and shoulders quite open (top right), the degree varying with the amount of curve you want on the ball. Swing as normal but along your body line, not the ball-to-target line. The club-face, must be aiming at the target.

It will also help to have the ball slightly further forward in the stance than usual. With a fade the ball will fly higher but less distance than a shot hit straight so take more club.

The opposite is true with a draw, a shot which moves from right to left in mid-air. This will need less club as the ball will fly lower. That, too, will be helped by having the ball slightly further back in your stance.

Once again, don't adjust your swing – adjust your set-up, aiming your feet and shoulders to the right of the target, though the clubface should be square to the target. Swing smoothly as normal.

There are occasions when you might need to hit the ball high, to get over a tree. Be realistic, making sure you have enough loft on the clubface to carry the top branches. If in doubt, play round the tree, taking an extra shot if necessary, rather than hitting the tree and maybe facing an even more difficult shot.

To hit the ball higher use a well lofted club and have the ball further forward in your stance. Also make sure most of your weight is on your

Left: To draw the ball stand more closed than normal, but still aim the clubface at the target.

Right: To fade the ball you must stand more open than normal, but aim the clubface at the target.

back foot, though don't lean back too far – you must stay balanced. Hold the very top of the grip as this will encourage more wrist action, which is necessary to whip the clubhead through. Take a long and slow swing making a very full turn on both the backswing and the follow-through.

To keep the ball low take a less lofted club and play the ball well back

Right: To hit the ball high have it forward in your stance and stand slightly open. Follow through fully.

Left: To hit the ball low have it back in your stance, stand slightly closed and swing smoothly. Use a less lofted club.

in your stance, also gripping further down on the club. Your weight should be more towards your left side. Restrict your swing to about three-quarters and also try to hold the follow-through to about the same length. At impact the hands must be leading the clubhead, dragging the club through impact.

125

Playing from rough

The rough often creates more difficulties for women than men as they lack the physical strength in their wrists and forearms to hit the ball hard enough to get it out of thick rough.

The best you can do is to use a very lofted club (the sand wedge is ideal), address the ball with an open stance and hit down into the back of it as hard as you can, hitting behind the ball.

There are times when you are close to the green and wish to control the ball from the rough whilst still carrying it over a bunker.

To achieve this stand slightly more open to encourage a higher, floating shot, grip down the club more, holding it tighter with the left hand than normal and address the ball further back in your stance.

Cock the wrists early in the back-swing, picking the club up more. Lead with the left hand coming down into impact and keep the left hand firm throughout the shot, finishing with a short but positive follow-through.